Soul Vagina

In between sex and God, who am I?

by Nomxolisi Ndlangana
"the queen"

ISBN:
ISBN-13: 978-0-9990897-1-2
ISBN-10: 0-9990897-1-4

This is for you love.

Contents

Special Thanks

I am beyond grateful to so many folks for this book. Left to our own devices, who knows where we would be, said my Brazilian friend, Fabiola Bergi, thank you for merely saying that line. Michael Kelly, for whom this book would still be a bunch of words on my laptop had you not come along and done literally everything, words fail me to express my gratitude. I must thank JD&J Design for stepping into my mind, deciphering my, at times abstruse thoughts, and creating a book cover I swoon over. Thank you to my older sister, Thobeka, my original number one fan. To my dear friend, Edgar Rodriguez, thank you for your consistent and unwavering encouragement towards all my artistic endeavors. To my dear friends, for keeping me alive when even writing had little oxygen, I thank you. I would be amiss if I didn't thank every man that has ever broken me down to a mess of chest-heaving crying, to you I owe nothing but offer gratitude. To K, thank you for reading everything I ever sent you with ardency and sobriety. My mother and family, thank you for keeping me. To every name unmentioned that has contributed positively in my life,

I beg your forgiveness and know that you are immortalized in my soul, truly. Thank You God. I wrote a book!

Entrance

I write for surely if I didn't, I would completely lose my mind and go crazy. I have for as long as my memory serves me well, found solace in writing. I have lost and found myself in writing.

I have been to Scotland's country side, swam across the English Channel, hunted with South Africa's lions and swayed in a trance at a club in Miami, all in one day in writing. I cursed the man who gave me life and loved him just as passionately in writing. I have killed my enemies violently in wars that have ravaged families, in writing. I have wept for myself, the girl I used to be, the young lady I was, the whore I repressed and the woman I didn't know I would become in writing. I have frolicked frivolously with men of all types carelessly, loved, hurt, broke to love again, all in writing. I have struggled with writing in writing. But writing, I have always had, loyal thou be, to thee I must thank. Because of you I have poetry, poetry that speaks of colorful pictures painted from prior periods professing love, wailing of swollen hearts, seducing with sex and all that is in between.

Nothing is required of you. Simply, pick up the wine, coffee or tea, read and just be.

Let it be known that I know that I am a dreamer. I am one of those people who dream and go crazy with their dreams. They are mine, free and there are no rules. There are times when I am by myself, I sit down and pretend that Oprah Winfrey is interviewing me about my book, Soul Vagina. Sometimes the Q & A goes a little like this:

Oprah: Why did you write this book?

Nomxolisi: Well, that's easy, I love to write. I was always compelled to write and when the Universe requires something of you, it will happen.

Oprah: Why this one, Soul Vagina?

Nomxolisi: Soul Vagina represents my relationship with my body, myself as a young woman and what I have experienced and learned about myself in romantic relationships. It is really an exploration about the complexities between two people in an intimate setting.

Oprah: Aha

Nomxolisi: It's a good read Oprah okay, it's a good read (laughing)...

Soul Vagina

The soul of my vagina begs moistly for your attention,

Feed it to its satisfaction your wholeness while I float to fantasy,

Tap against the walls and delight at their crumbling,

sink into the murky pool

of my soul vagina

and let your firmness be baptized,

get lost in the deep of my eyes

and let words take the form of our actions

while the soul of my vagina goes through a reawakening,

the soul

of my vagina

goes through a reawakening.

This piece was the beginning of what would become an inquiry

into the complexities between two people in an intimate

relationship. And so, it began...

SEX IS DEATH

Sex is not an act of kindness,

When done right

It is a compromise of protection,

A demise of demeanor

A demonic spirit of rambunctious indulgence

That leads a soul to seek penance

For succumbing to being possessed by a cock and not no

chicken flock sort of stock,

The real deal wrapped in skin so tight

It's a fitting cover for this hard lover;

He has a reputation for slippin' deep

Into crevices that used to be dormant volcanoes of murky

waters

And dead emotions,

From oceans of bastards who left you cold and alone,

He warms your soul with a flow unknown to your pretty tight

missy,

That's when the hissing is insisting on oozing out your lips

Invigorating a gyrating of hips,

He is driving you to a place poets scribe of on days divine

inspiration reveals to them;

This is not a man having sex

Reinventing or bettering sex,

Lest he has become the very act,

It is in you,

Confusing and polluting your body with a purifying and

elevating disease;

You're heaving and convulsing in space and time

While your mind has entered a liberty not of this world,

Word,

You have been introduced to sex.

Anything before this was a test

Nothing short of a holistic preparation for a grand master

conquest of uncharted stratospheres.

Now breathe lady

He is here.

And give it all you've got

Because today you die

And It's quite alright.

Ingest this nirvana

And die because

Sex, when done right is death.

"Life will do this thing, this crippling, debilitating thing where it tosses you around rag doll style until you are convinced that love has no room for you. Then one day, ever so suddenly something happens and it occurs to you so sweetly that it just may be that you were wrong."

THIS WAS HIM (A TRAIN)

There he was placating his energy all over the damn place,

So unassuming,

Commanding every panty to wet itself,

Buckle knees

And freeze

And never saying so much as a "hello",

Who the fuck was this?!

His fitted forced my head to dip to catch his dark eyes

That held on to his childhood sweetness yet still rung of a man

that would flip 180 easy if you stepped too far left,

As if fighting was a gift he had to survive the streets;

He was hard,

His physique suggested a tough left hook;

Flipping back and forth between this man and the world,

He stood there so quietly

Yet owned the room like the ancient tribal warriors that

caused, suspended and ended riots,

He might,

I just know it,

He might raise his majestic hand fiercely right up to my

exposed neck

Grab it

let the air escape

And catch it with his full mouth,

Because he'd only hurt me enough for me to like it,

This was him,

On my morning commute to a nine-to-five poison

He spilled the cure for my loneliness, futility and servitude

With his existence,

This was him,

My womb danced in celebration,

My soul found solace in his existence and I couldn't help

myself but to just stare;

I had no words for this divine revelation created for my

elation, sedation and peace,

We left the world behind us

All of us

Except no one saw him but I and I;

The noise, the rush, the hub of underground fell silent

And he rose to meet me with his lips

And a deadly kiss.

If he was trouble,

I wanted it.

If he were a demon

Paralyze me.

If he were booze

I'd have him till I passed out on this train maimed by the vice.

This was him.

The man for me.

1 2 5th swallowed him whole...

'Stand Clear of the Closing Doors'

And just like that he was gone.

My robust, psychological, loving mother f-er, giver of Peggy

Lee's kinda fever.

I know he's out there

That was him.

Life becomes a little easier because I know he exists.

MY LESBIAN

I'm no lesbian

I just like you

she said to me.

I smiled.

She was beautiful,

funky fro kinks longer than I could ever imagine mine to be,

Sitting on her chocolate skin she wished I could peel,

But you see

I know me

And I could never do to her everything I wanted to do to you.

I could never bury my body into hers the way I would with you.

And You,

Swinging around these streets like king Kunta,

wetting my peach

Leave me sweating your knob,

I could knock for hours,

Pass out

And pick up from the last lick I locked on your glock,

Amen. I always pray for you.

My tongue synchronize swimming in an ocean of white lush,

Summoning the rush,

I imagine I'd be there days if you let me dare,

To be fair,

I'd need to rest,

Before I began the rest.

I saw the vision of our spiritual revolution born through our

physical revelations,

We're only capable of deep sensations according to our divine

creation,

I was designed to align with your nude might tonight,

So my body has chunky soft bags of tricks and tests,

With an end game - how good can I make this man feel,

How long will I whine over you before I shoot you to a new

moon of ecstasy?

See, I'm no lesbian either

Though under the right light I might light your fire

I said to her,

But I have a magnetic addiction to this bearded creation,

and the only affliction I'm hoping for involves mounting a

black stallion that was lord in Sparta

and king in Africa,

Black magic ya

I'm a star when I sing for ya,

I'm a vampire when I come for ya

I'm a giver when I spill for ya

If only for one day,

Just one

Let me be all the woman you ever needed,

I would be yours:

Bosom to cup your tears

Tits to feed your soul,

I'd pass out limp and still say yes,

Because you are a bless,

Born and already passed every test.

So, to the phly chic with the sleek feel

Bless you little lady

But my body belongs to a man

And to man,

I beg

Best come take me

Before my heart gives life to angels

Or you will never know the glory of my African pussy.

That, I would wish on no man.

How I Love

Allow me to synchronize visual imaginations of venereal body

demonstrations,

Mister,

petitions of pleas from strangers, lovers and dudes driving

Range Rovers

To bowl me over

have never left my phone,

Not at all to be honored;

It's no mistake that I've managed to stay sober

'Cause you are my liquor

So I'm going to need you to inebriate a sister.

And you're also what mama might call a looker,

So could easily make me a certified Nevada or is it Nebraska

hooker.

Nonetheless,

Make me your lover.

I have a soliloquy in mind

That I'd like to deliver with a dose of Swiss sweets stashed

secretly in cavernous, biological constructions,

You have my full permission to pursue its soulful destruction,

I can tell you need no instructions

Or some sort of induction,

You understand the sole function

of your pick

Is to dig deep into every space I occupy.

You begin your plight

With a smile tailed with a graze on my waist

laced with enough explosives to cripple my walk for days;

I can feel the vim of your stirring ways,

Since you walked in,

I've been hoping for so much as a kiss

to release me into a temporary state of bliss.

Shit.

Mister please,

Confer with the gods,

Give it pause

But if this night ends with an empty bed

and my hand imagining your head in my dreams again,

Well, let this wine drown me now

Out the mental misery of you

Into a drunken slumber of black.

I tell you now,

If your roots don't find a home in my garden,

Then I seek the silence of death to quiet the howls of my body

for the company of yours,

Than to miss just even a kiss.

Because when you kiss,

Well...

I smell roses on mars,

Heaven takes a break from the sky

Comes down and settles in between my thighs,

I'm convinced the Greek gods gifted you with lips that dip into

hips,

Operating like you're expecting tips

And banning me to land of addicted to the flow of your soul.

I wouldn't be shocked if you rocked me steady,

To flip me like jelly,

Feel you in my belly

Undo my buttons I think I'm ready,

Anything baby,

I will sin all over you

And pray you kill me kindly

And before you blind me

I'll remind you there won't ever be any like me.

And we'll wake on a Sunday morning

For our souls to save

Because of how we misbehaved.

My friends want to know

What I think it's like,

I say,

it's like

When I take the mic

and spit a wet set of deep rhymes

met with you coming up my stage

and congratulating my victory

With your sickening poetry.

Mister,

What I'm saying is,

She is addicted to him,

I love you

And the rest of me

Needs you.

So make a decision,

Is it going to be me

or her?

"I paid attention to every sound, smell and feel of my body as it spoke quietly but loud enough for him to dance to the melody of my song. I learned him, remembered him and loved the us we were."

PART 1 - LOVE INQUIRY

There really is no way to start a conversation like this,

If you need to order a drink or take a piss,

I suggest you take a second before I begin this,

Because once I go,

Not even God's hand could stop this flow.

I commonly populate stages

But this is no show

Because Nono don't do shows,

I prefer to epitomize and personify poetry in its jarring beauty,

And for you to understand my frenzy

I have to take you back to Thursday night at the pantry,

When he got so close to me he could smell the sex sweating out

my pores,

I was perspiring lust;

He'd been so good to me for so long

Marinated my thighs with his drool and made me look like a fool

As I groaned a deep long "ooh,"

and watched me get high

Prepping me for the ultimate ride;

Like tithes

He gave to me like he believed

I would be the one to save his soul from the hordes of empty

birds that circled his dock.

Now, I have been everything under a man's hands,

but with his hands

Pressed firmly against my chest

I must confess,

I had never been fucked or loved before

Until I met this man.

He infected me with his love making,

And morphed his body into a cure,

Affecting me like some spiritual lure,

I was sure he was some god sent to resurrect a part of me I thought

had died after countless nights of unforgiving loneliness

Lord, he crippled with his sexiness

But this time,

I had no inclination to fight

the vortex that palpitated only for his dong,

I let him take his time as I grew into a restless beast that swore

to do as he pleased

Just please,

Ease that thing into the scheme of things,

By things,

I mean me,

ease that beast into me

And if I scream don't you dare cease,

Wait till my slit melts into seas;

It wasn't the glory of its dark hardness suctioned tight by thy

pussy highness,

It's how he sang love songs with his cock,

as his hands knead into my skin searching for symptoms of arousal,

How he spilled secrets with his back flexing, complex *dickmatizing*

injections,

My body was split into sections of exploration,

To be bruised by affections,

skin wet from sweat and tongues surging,

And he covered all ground

Came around

Touch down two, three, ooh wee,

Four times,

four times I cried stifled by this black revelation.

He liked me,

He loved me

And it wasn't enough to just fuck me

he pined to wake up with me

To talk about nothing and everything in between as we cooled

down by the morning breeze.

I wanted his dick to live inside of me.

I mean, like occupy my vaginal space on a permanent basis.

For this jock I sang a song,

"I know, the universe created you for my womb, so

Can your dick, can your dick, can your dick

live inside of me?"

At this point I'd lost my damn mind

But that's alright,

You see,

When a man happens to you the way he did,

You've got to slowly to pull down your panties

And respond to his physical inquiry with the same level of

honesty and ruthlessness,

So, once I had recovered

What I did,

Well, there is no room for what I did in Part 1...now part 2...

Ain't nothing but love.

You can hear their strained whispers

Full of jealous glimmers

As they watch me stride on by,

They don't seem to understand

why he just doesn't seem to care

About their cushioned chests

Advertised like fake treasure chests,

Or their bargained for booties mounted on their backs bopping

for the highest bidder.

They like to bend over,

all over themselves they tend to fall over,

I giggle

They are the kind that tickle,

It's all a little too funny;

Some often wonder,

others dream of it

and a few ask me,

I tell '*em*,

honey pull up a chair and get comfortable

'cause mama's about get explicitly bare.

This here is an education for the woman,

nymphs, whores, sluts prohibited,

nymphs, whores, sluts in a woman

have a seat

and have a look here see...

First,

You must, dust to dust, you must

rid you of your fear,

it only cripples and there can be no sexual ripples,

Two,

lights on, dim low,

look him straight dead deep depth in eyes

and say

"Hi Ty,

tonight, I am going to transform the relationship of your cock

to my pussy,

In fact, we'll start by calling her Lucy

'cause she's about to get a lot more juicy,"

Do you feel me?

Ladies, please stay with me...

Next, we pause

not for no dramatic applause,

we pause for the bigger bulge,

Then we lick,

slow, deliberate, moist we lick,

Your legs spread in split, strong in stance

Watch him watch you trickle wetness

down your gentle slope

And observe his happiness

inspired by his sexiness,

Watch him want you

and need you

he'll want to eat you

Tonight and every other night

whether you're in or out of sight,

is that alright?

Now go love him

full to the brim

surrender to him

hell, even fuck him

But

make sure

your body is the extension of his impression,

So be he a sexy Harlem or Brooklyn or Bronx brother,

To your mother

best give him all that sugar,

really get him to know ya,

So he can remember

You are to be his only lover.

frolic freakishly

yes please

fuck feverishly

yes please

hell say bless thee!

and when he loves you harder and deeper

And I have no choice words in my pot

I simply turn to my girl Jill Scott

and sing song,

'doo doo doo doo doo doo I need you'

And if he sends you to Timbuktu

take it like a woman,

if he has you screaming "ooh"

take it like a woman

if he has you forgetting your name,

forget your name, get a new name

and take it like a woman!

And by the end of it all

Truth be told all in all.

He'll be past curled toes and breathless moans,

Because you would have elevated him to a whole new whole.

Now take that man's hand

make him understand

Let him know

how from now on it's going to go,

that this here is the gold

that don't ever wear old.

Let this be the lesson,

that with you

it ain't nothing,

it ain't nothing but love.

Ain't That Some Shit

His hands summoned my waist with an enticing violence

for the rest of me to move towards his beast,

he smelled like a royal feast;

I was heated and thirsty

and he knew I'd be knocking for his coming

and lo and behold,

there I was,

knocking with my lips and I wasn't looking for no tips

and whatever is in between my hips was on fire.

I'd be a liar

if I said I didn't want to participate in a dirty romp of sexual

nuances between body parts,

let's make art if that's what you want.

Mind you, this is not a sex piece,

See, his voice bellowed beneath my skin like ripples on a quiet sea,

it seemed that our disconnect with time led to inexplicable

sensations

that sedated doubts and buts,

inducing a self-contained high as his mouth played with

personal pieces of my canvas,

And some spirit of sort for lack of a better thought

pressed my desire to deliver better pleasures to my one-time

lover;

And for a split second, I could hear my sister saying,

"Stay away from men such as this brother"

but her voice dissolved quickly into the cacophony of

chemistry between fella and me,

his African bella.

My roots are drenched deep,

born and bred from mother Africa's wild and dangerous

bosom,

My tender hips and my soft lips rile up easy when attacked by

a lion

and he came charging,

I was never a tame dame, just a lady;

yes, I succumbed to his stealth and purred

as he groped

whispering with his eyes,

inviting with his fingers,

titillating with his breath,

this was a spiritual meth

but the math did not add up,

he had someone and I was someone broken

yet he was stitching me back together with each motion,

he crowned me his queen

and killed me to deliver me to my heaven

Amen.

I loved him where she couldn't reach

and he elevated me from a concubine

into an aged wine

he valued as his highest prized.

He ruined me that night

and he did it just right.

I can still feel him inside of me on lonely nights when even the

warm body beside me has proved that it likes me;

He morphed into a scar in my mind that will never heal

because when the sun comes up

it brings light to truth that was hidden in a cloud of passion,

and mine was

he was one night,

everything I needed and nothing that I could ever have,

Should I have left when he first foot step,

Yes.

Because broken is a state of transition that must be embraced

with meditation,

it's my damn trepidation that led to this man,

and even though he loved me good and hard,

it is now hard for me, my heart and my delicate parts

because truth is,

he was

just

a

one night stand...

Ain't that some shit?

Black

Black,

You, creamy chocolate creature creeping up on me at the light

of day,

your mahogany rustic scent

buckles my knees;

Black,

your charcoal veil blinds me in love;

Black,

You, sexy color of all,

take away bumps and bring out silhouettes.

Black,

life began with you

and that is why they hate you;

Black,

You, bold brother of ballers

bring me some of that black magic

and rub against my caramel;

Black,

every night I go to bed with you,

and every night you hit the jackpot,

Sometimes you take me on journeys

but every night you never disappoint,

Black,

you are the void that fills me up.

Black,

two sugars, no cream please,

that's how I take it,

Black.

"Positive affirmations are a reflection of you, what they do from then on is what they do. Rest easy."

SING FOR ME

Write me a song baby.

I sat on his lap like a good little girl,

I'd been good

Saved the bad for his song,

I'd waited so long for,

My lips were hot plates of ripe plumpness

Ready to be a mess,

I was burning with sass,

All I wanted

Was a melody

That would make me forget

Any historic regret

Or lover I cursed with a knife or bat;

My eyes hummed a tune hoping to inspire this mother fucker

To be the kind of monster

That amnesia-induces a sister

Into forgetting fuck ups that lead countless startups,

So, I took a deep breath

Like I was on some type of meth,

And asked,

Write me a song baby,

Sing for me.

I was sure his fineness had earned him title "highness",

But he'd never had a home-grown princess

Explain his greatness

With words that mimic lyrical prowess;

Look at me,

Have you seen yourself of late?

A tan that fans pay grands for

You wear with a natural flair,

Forever more I offer you my womb

Just pick a room,

You smell like the man God said is made for my bed,

an eloquent depiction of a thug with no record;

And from the way you move,

I can tell your sexual groove is far from the blues.

Mister, you are sexy,

Your stillness excites my mentality,

Intellectually I'm constantly titillated

If they banned liquor,

I'd hide you in between parts of me,

I am foolishly intoxicated by you,

I won't give you up;

So come on,

I've been so good,

I have it bad,

Write me a song baby,

Sing for me.

Sing.

Priceless

They say that I don't like sex, don't want sex,

See that makes no sense,

You see,

my vagina is the gold that has that 70-year-old man in Africa

spending his days filtering through sand, sticks and stones for,

It is that rock of diamond that has men crashing craniums for,

killing for,

It is the pot of gold Troy went down for,

The gem that stems from genesis

and the canal that births life, sin and death

Yes,

so if I dish it out like a dollar candy,

how much value can I really attach now Randy?

I know it's worth every bit of your

time,

smiles,

calls,

texts,

your gifts

because when I surrender my jewels at your feet,

The Heavens take a break from the sky,

come down

and settle in between my thighs,

the best thing since French fries;

Get to enjoy its delights

and take your time,

I become the sweetest fruit of the seed of time,

I let you be

Until you are full

and I am empty,

and all we have left is time,

Time to do it all over again

and again

and again...a moment please...

and again,

Wide in deep tight,

It's all right.

They say that I don't want sex, don't like sex,

Perplexed?

That just makes no sense.

Love is made once again

They always want to,

make me feel good

From the moment they meet me,

greet me,

Definitely,

They want to make love to me,

And so it begins,

As lips cushion lips and I am baptized by his mouth,

His hands curiously exploring every dip and curve on my terrain,

Making deliberate delays down my plain,

I'm arching my back thrusting my chest deeper into the sultry hollows of his mouth,

Sweet moisture spilling out of me as honey from a comb,

Spreading limbs into splits spewing pleasure inviting tender caress,

His limber tongue gives me the wettest of joys,

And all I can think,

Is to stop,

Before love is made

Once again.

"Not making love or having sex may be exactly the love you need to give yourself to ultimately experience the unspeakable pleasure the universe has for you."

My one-time lover

I sometimes slip into that honey sweet-like dream that I lived

with you that night,

We laughed hard into the melting silence

That engulfed us in its grandeur,

your limbs flowed with professional precision

as you summoned me with your body,

I had no time to waste on what if's or no's,

My biology swelled and emitted heat

Proclaiming my excitement,

Second after second, silently I begged

Your hands to never leave my surface

And I prayed your mouth to continue to be against me,

Every breath I eased out sank me deeper into your love-dungeon,

As I felt your power grow in strength on my rear

As you lay bare behind me,

Your hands and fingers gyrated on my breasts,

I hardened at the feel of your close proximity and your kind hands,

I succumbed myself completely,

Patient as you slowly surprised me with what you did to me,

As you felt me

More and more and more...

The mind sex had been caressing me long before you knew the inside of my blouse-

Your smart lines with your seasoned mind kissed my naive brain matter,

And the more you spoke of science and politics,

The quicker my clothes came off in my mind

And you lay in between my ride,

So, this moment,

Naked as we be,

Has been in the making since you never spoke to me of it;

Mister, you are a pleasant passing surprise,

This I know

But before you leave,

I will forget that I ever loved any other man

and you will be the first, last and

My One-Time Lover.

The Morning After

You are invited to my cavernous crevice to explore

Discover

And celebrate,

To attend to the business of your growth

While you satisfy us

As you excite and bless my sensitivities

And splash your joy on my sacred walls,

I am pleased that you are my guest tonight;

Hello,

My name is Nina

a.k.a. vagina.

Cherries and Poetry

The letters line up in formation,

Salute their master

And spring to him fever-filled,

He breathes life into each and every single letter,

They explode onto my flesh and rush through my blood;

I try to find my letters so I can give him words

But the ball of sweetness in my mouth has spoken before me

and his words have been reduced to rhythmic sounds of

onomatopoeia,

We carried on as animals trapped in a cage

Fervently waiting for that moment,

As people with minds secretly conspiring;

That night, I was the cherry in the drink for the taking,

he was the cherry in my mouth dancing about,

And we were poetry

In those moments of safe silence.

"Live in moments for they become pivotal points in life strung together with time to become memories that make or break you."

IN MY DREAM

Pour me some sweet tea pea

And best you quit looking at me

Like I am the fusion of allurement

And perpetual vaginal excitement,

At best,

That's what I call a clear case of enticement

And I'd be obliged to invite your soul to dark holes

Of enlightenment;

I am a self-professed goddess of royal Greek seas,

A rose,

Always in season,

Seasoned in sex, loving and giving;

I offer blessed men

Spiritual revivals induced by quiet sexual advances,

Peep the hips,

And you think it's what you could do to these hips,

Yet this is a ship you can't rock without your head getting rocked hard to death by my sail,

See, these seven seas in me will drown you,

Captain or no captain,

You'd be captivated by the tightest slice money couldn't buy

under the knife by thousand dollar hands;

From the cusp of breasts,

Supple and succulent,

Trailing to the weight of my rear,

Firm and ferocious in its back-it-up feat,

To the heat your seed would meet

At the initial pistol insertion,

It's all real.

And this is the deal:

I reeled you in the moment I dreamed you in my visions;

Made unspoken petitions to the gods

To deliver a lord of men,

Conceived from grace,

Marine strong

And cock long enough to unlock America's generation,

And addicted to Nono's elation.

From praying and silent meditating,

I had you before

I made you work to get me.

So don't tell me you fucked the shit out of me,

You are the concept of a poet

That was born in my dreams.

You came because I said so.

Sugar in the Raw

Yes you are, the cane sugar in a human body,

I do want to lick and roll my tongue around that stick,

Soak up the juices while the rest trickles down my chin;

Nothing quite like the sweetness of a raw sugar cane stick,

You swagger-bounce like a god of some kingdom

Everywhere you strut

Leaving me to catch my jaw

As I watch from afar,

Now what is a girl to do

When a man just has it

But to simply take and have it,

And I'm working baby -

From the natural flick of my hair

To the lean in to grab that pen

All the way down to the slight rise of my skirt

As I swing the left to the right of my thigh,

Every move,

On one mission,

To seduce the sweetness off of your body

Down on to my open flesh

And seep right back into mother earth that created your perfect,

Yes, perfect you are

For how else could sugar cane in a human body be,

But simply

raw and perfect.

HE SAID SHE SAID

He said, I'm his only number one sweet lover,

He said, I'm the light in his life type a sister

And he said, he could never find another

But he forgot about the baby mama

Sleeping underneath his covers.

I loved me some Jerome Jaden Franklin,

His lies felt like love letters to a lover you didn't want to murder

with blades of rendezvous with other beaus,

No telling who was more screwed,

Me is probably the truth

'Cause I knew,

He was a seed that never grew,

Old and grown at 32,

He drilled deep with his dips

And my ears, eyes and hips

Said 'yes please'

I'll take some chips with those fibs

But I loved this man

So any fact that meant friction I faked as fiction,

I wasn't ready to give up this *dicktion*,

Dicktion with a K,

So I stayed and stayed and he always came,

He said, I'm his only number one sweet lover,

He said, I'm the light in his life type a sister

And he said, he could never ever find another

But he forgot about the baby mama

Sleeping underneath his covers.

When you discover that you ain't his only lover,

It's almost like an infection on the liver

System failures all over

Affecting your behaviors,

Soul sister with good manners

Flips to bold bitch

Come closer you might slip into a ditch,

I'm not the cursing type

But I was ripe with mother-f'ers

And quickly got on the call with

His Christian mother

Asking what type o' father created this monster,

I, I, I, love you baby baby b-b-baby,

Stuttering as if the breaks in between letters

would concert a better novela,

I'd had enough of my liar,

Smoking the ganja

Song in my head got louder...

Yo, J, I got something to say,

That's a whole lot of bullshit

So when he said,

I'm the only one that's in his head,

I cried and I laughed hard

'Cause I knew what is true,

That's a whole lot of bullshit.

So, I watered the seed,

He didn't think I'd leave

And now he screams in his sleep when he sings for a lost queen.

DINNER NEVER CAME

It's not like I was waiting for a meal to come

but it never came

And I still came.

With T,

I liked the idea of sipping tea making love to him more than the

actual thing happening.

In my mind.

See, he was the epitome of a perfect lover,

His piece fit into my chest

And at best

Orchestras played symphonies at Heaven Hall,

Cellos hard hitting my walls,

Where fancy plates decked with caviar and lobster served as

food,

It was so damn good,

I lapped him up in ecstatic motions

Summoning dormant oceans

To drown me on dry land,

His entirety needed to stay in me,

His warmth was never too hot just right,

Heat, flex, stretch, arch that back,

Sigh

Aye

And I hadn't even got on the ride

Yet already I was ripe to slide,

Instantly it almost seemed

Things peaked to steamed!

He was so nice to me.

He beamed at my black skin

Kissed my soft skin,

Said he liked my skin so soft.

He smiled,

I laughed.

He got so close,

He let his breath kiss my neck before he blessed with his

mouth.

All I could feel was the volatile vibrations down my south,

I was hungry,

I mean famished,

I was ready to rip at seams

And climb beams

To get a piece of his piece,

Fire that bazooka

Make sure you kill me dead

Down

Fuck underground

If I'm found

Alive

I'm coming hard for you.

He played with breasts and I fixed the mess in his head

With my spoken word

Ooh wee he'd make me sing for him

And it was exactly what needed to be.

What I'm saying is,

Dinner was never late,

It just never came.

And that's okay.

Deep In

As I pressed the palms of my hands on to his bare back

And dug my paws into his flesh,

Vision blinded by black,

He put in a request for my poetry,

Not some poetry

But my poetry,

Without thought

I knead into his flesh with my knuckles

While my words caressed his spirit

Into alignment with his body

Putting us both in a mood

Defined by sensuality;

As I gave this man my healing,

He gave me his attention

Commanding my ultimate submission,

And it took only his listening

To my vulnerability, my insanity and my words

And I was in...deep in.

"My gutter is a dark, dirty rendition of an

American horror love story. Once I am there, it's

devils and ghouls dragging me down as I endeavor

to survive the disservice of a lover. It ain't pretty."

He's Leaving Me

His bags are packed,

plastic bags in hand

with the trash he'll probably try to cash,

Shoes, boots and all,

Papers, documents and any piece he deems his,

Packed from the rack,

Today, he is leaving me.

The car is pulling up to take him away from me

And I need to make my last stand against his angst;

I jerk the heels off my feet, fall to the floor landing in a pang that

has me gasping,

And there I begin my procession of pleas,

Hands in prayer to hands at the hem of his pants

I fixed many a time

To crawling trailing the tears that teetered before me,

asking, begging, convincing, watching,

As he dragged me along with him trying to get away from me,

Refusing to look down at the woman he loved,

He was leaving me

And even as the concrete tore at my knees

I held on,

Even as the cab driver left his lower half of his jaw on the floor

at the sight of my desperation,

I held on;

He dropped his jazz in the trunk,

Looked down and shook the rest off of his ankle,

I sat there, lay there, cried there,

Reminisced there and things in between I did there,

On that front yard

That was once ours,

He was no longer leaving me,

He had left me.

And now to move on

As the one left behind.

MAID OF MEN

How many of them have I met?

Loved?

Enough,

to coarsen the skin on my bones to that of unvarnished wood,

prickly at the sides, so coarse I've become,

I've come to accept that I could be a muse for a painter perhaps,

broken and beautiful,

alone and loving,

smiling and cold;

I fold,

Did so when the last man I draped with love,

loved me until they needed me no more,

I'd fed them,

fortified them,

Pleased them,

Held them,

laughed with them,

spent for them

'till the earth's axis tilted to deliver new blessings in their lives and suddenly I became less of a necessity

and more of a complicated broad embroiling his peace,

His precious peace that I dug out from the earth with my hands,

feet, tears and sweat,

mountain-moving prayers I Fedex'd to the Lord daily

to have mercy on these humanly creations

And now here we are!

In a cockpit of random acts of kindness

spurred by my begging;

Yes, I have had to beg for them to show some sweetness,

they did for a short while

perhaps plagued by guilt or gratitude

never quite knew

but it was always so short-lived,

the sweetness.

I would soon find myself empty again

curled in a ball inside of myself

wondering if I was expected to surrender every part of my life

in exchange for a thank you and a poetic compliment?

Was I the maid of men,

to be used to fix broken fixtures in their lives and expected to

quietly gather my rosebuds at the end of their plight

and discreetly exit using the back door

making sure to not make a fuss or show of it all?

When they looked at me,

Did they see strength that needed no shoulder

or did they not think of me at all?

Did they contemplate me as a "situation" with their brothers in

phone and bar conversations,

a needy little thing that did too much

or was there no thought to begin with?

Or was I a complimentary hot plate, a good fuck and a nice little girl

that fell in love with wolves and had no idea.

I felt them all,

all those things I thought in moments of quiet,

I felt them as their unforeseen egos grabbed their necks

egging them on to ignore my sensibilities,

reduced to text messages sending well wishes as I swam up my

tide

vomiting water trying to stay afloat

swimming to survive the night

alone,

ignored as I asked for little pleasures that appeased my romantic

heart;

trying hard for one day was the general game

to soon resolve back to what mattered most to them,

And there it was!

The rolling revelation that jolts the spirit up to attention!

ATTENTION WOMAN!

You are not important.

They will never move mountains to see you smile,

they will never give up too much so you can have a little,

they will never do what means nothing to them

and everything to you,

you are a yield sign on their way to their stop sign.

It must be then,

It must be true

as I examine who I have been and what they have done for me,

it must be my truth,

I must be the maid of men.

Made to scrub the blood off their walls from gone-by lovers,

to lick their wounds in my bed

as their heads cradled my bosom, lactating my power to strengthen themselves,

availing myself at any hour should their cries come knocking on my doorstep,

saving them from the ugly corners of the city that seduced young men every day,

and fucking them good for good measure.

Except it was more of an emptying of my soul 'till my ovaries had no life left

to give is more of what I did.

I only expected very little,

no money, no gifts, no wild adventures tagged with thousands of dollars,

just simple little things

that meant nothing to them

and everything to me.

With each passing week I noticed my little pleasures dissipating into forgotten suggestions by me,

he was whispering in my ear,

you are a maid,

maid of men.

"To know who you are means you can always get back to yourself when anyone pummels you to an emotional pulp. There is something greater waiting for you once you get back to you."

Matrix

There really is no way to begin a piece such as this,

Words are a painstaking attempt to depict a private moment in

a life

that could change the public perception of a sexual relationship;

I was in fight mode from the get go,

So his "hello" was met with "no"

No you will not spit some game

About the shape of my frame

Hose me down with tricky lyrics to some song I never heard

And turn me into a singing bird

For a moment's pleasure.

I could not have been more wrong.

It wasn't long before I knocked on my knees with pleases for deeds

he performed in dark suites lit with fire from inside my empire

Now,

Pleasure, dictionary defined might imply what I felt was in line,

I must disagree,

To the highest degree,

I protest because of this

I must insist you listen to each word,

I birth

And deliver in this space

So you might begin to taste this unnamed euphoria that trips

my steps at random intervals during my day:

I could see his face as I rode out dreams, frustrations and all

that was out my gut,

Clenching abs released streams of stress

Translated as orgasmic tremors,

Unmatched by prior interactions,

I was in a daze of love with a fool who turned a pool into an ocean

of *cumming*,

Summoning extreme joys with his strong toy,

At some point I lost his face,

And I could no longer feel the source of my pleasure,

My body had become the very ocean he dipped his hand,

I had become the verb,

I was lost,

This mother f-er had reintroduced my body to myself,

Hello? I am you

And you are beautiful to the point of extinction.

I had never been done like this,

Seen in such capacity,

And he saw me in time zones

To me and people,

Men and women alike were unknown,

I was in Zion under his hand,

Gave up my mind at his command,

because I was in a matrix

And he was the key to the fix

I believed.

He was blue, green and red pill,

there was no going back or forward

just the here and now.

SINCE THEN

Now,

Myself and I,

I'm no kiss and tell kind a gal

But for the exception of mankind

I cannot decline a crowd's invitation

To satisfy an already inclination

To bust this door wide open,

And yes ladies and gentlemen,

Absolutely pun intended.

My story is made for virgins still satisfied by their own hand,

for men leading with mediocrity in such a complex situation

such as a sexual relation,

For women misled by broken relationships,

And stupid kids skidding hard

Hoping for an orgasmic punch

Not realizing

That slaying a pussy perfectly hard

Needs a delicate touch

To attain the incomparable concoction of climax, calamity and

closure.

Because ladies and gentlemen

When you've done it right

Gawdamnit!

You die

You fly dismally into the open skies,

Upon which you are swallowed wide

To a white abyss of closure.

I cried.

You see for me,

He found me.

They always find you,

So quit looking ladies because they find you,

Hunched over a beverage he used as leverage,

No soul should be drinking vodka and coke,

He switched me to something a little less confusing,

Which opened the door to what would become the biggest,

grandest score

Of all time,

I was now in the company of a gentleman

And my wet panties were a symptom of his chivalry and deep

scent,

That ignited sex,

I was vexed

And he must've been wearing axe

Because just like the ad

By him I was to be had.

First, he played with his eyes

He was nice

I never knew the roll of his dice

He hit me with fire and ice

Fucking me with words over dinner,

By dessert he had me past eager,

I'd already worked out my plan on what to deliver,

I just didn't plan for his counter offers;

When I'd drenched his pick with spit

He spit a jive that switched the vibe

To a moaning crooner,

To only hush me delicately;

His hand cupped my mouth

I licked his palm

Between candle-lit giggles and finger glides over mine,

I'd turned into certified concubine

I wanted to taste him

Completely

Continuously

At all angles, positions

And times,

I grind, he smiled

He drove for miles

Switching gears and making every *gawdamn* turn,

He earned every head bop and jaw lock,

His cock clock set the time of death,

Our breaths were in precise unison

And like a lady I gave in,

So, he eased his soul into the depths of my conforming cavernous

creation,

Baiting elation

I was shaking

Fucking shaking

And just as I took my last breath,

His mouth caught the air

That took me there,

Held onto my bare body

As my spirit left it.

I, cried.

And as I lay nude on that bed,

Wailing under the cooling effects of post perfect sex

He didn't need to ask,

About the tears

Because he knew

Like I did too

That he had just *slay'd* this pussy,

So like the gentleman he was,

He pecked a sweet one on my right

Held me for a moment

Then left me to enjoy the light.

And since then,

I gave up late nights on the West side

I prefer down South now.

UNTITLED

I knew this day would come

when the piss, mess and stress from having met you

would culminate to a perfect piece of poetry

fit for parading my erotic pain on a stage for listeners to lean in

and breathe in this piece

and hopefully I won't go home tonight to slip another pill to skip

the pain

that hits hardest against my chest amidst the silence during bed

rest,

So, here goes:

To say that we fucked would be a brutal waste of words,

my vocabulary may not be a match for... say a Jay Z protégé

but I can appreciate my humble linguistic abilities to poetize a

sentence, make it sound like an event an audience might believe

they once participated in,

So, no

we did not just fuck.

We met,

his hands came and introduced themselves to my body like an old lover from another life

that remembered how to excite sensibilities that lead to explosions of waterfalls inside my tower,

He slipped the pieces of cloth that covered me off

and bathed the space in between my thighs with his sweet sweat,

Yes, his sweat was sweet,

ask me how I know?

A lady does not say she likes to blow.

He was buttering me up for the oncoming traffic of solid gratification,

He belonged inside of me

and my walls caved in and around him

confirming my original thoughts

that him and I were right.

Now, I think I might have died when he moved the flow of my performance to lock legs on necks,

mind you, his eyes never left mine

as if the flames of passion in my pupils hardened his joy even further.

We spoke in beckoning moans and animalistic groans,

he was hurting me and I like it unashamed I even cried

"more?" he implored, "yes please," I widened my door.

I lost myself in this man,

I was good at that: losing myself.

As a matter of fact,

he inspired the limber mistress hidden in this soul sister,

to flip the script in those sheets,

I gripped his waist into a deadlock,

"alright, now watch me, this is how you ride,"

I conditioned him,

It wasn't ego just a natural, instinct he evoked by the way he

was loving on me,

we plateaued tirelessly into a spent state of cacophonous,

coming contentment.

Sprawled nude on my bed,

I giggled,

he chuckled.

We both knew we had actively just participated in what might

go down in history as a revolutionary fucking session,

if it was depression I was experiencing prior to his meeting

he doctored that disease,

And this was how he was every single time,

he made sure I got there and again and one more time

just because he could

and I took care to repay his endeavors

with my own measure of artistic, sensual gestures.

we were like a raw footage of pornographic inspiration,

Monster's Ball if you can imagine

minus the booze and broken bits between the two participants.

I should've known it wouldn't have lasted

maybe because my pussy was born to bless dicks and leave them

hoaxed

so, the owners grab their coats and make for the door,

Or maybe I really was the slut he said I was for spreading so fast,

but nah,

grandma wed her first night rendezvous going strong thirty

years through.

So, then what happened that was so bad that you couldn't stay?

Could I have not loved the pain away?

Or was I just a passing phase?

I hate to think that I was a vixen victualing a void your woman

might have left

and maybe she came back

so I had to pack my bags and leave your sack.

The issue is

my ex-lover,

I never told you this but uh,

I loved you.

My vagina still tries to find you on wet nights vibrating viciously

seeking to be tamed by you

like only you could.

I guess I'm better off right?

Probably dodged a bullet they like to say?

I suppose this is the story I will tell my soul

'till your wound finds itself tucked away with the rest of its kind

and I can move on to sex better than I ever did

because apparently what doesn't kill you

makes you stronger, better

and might I add wetter.

So, for my future lover,

I say,

buckle up baby

because I broke and almost died

but I survived and I am alive,

And somewhere in between the celibacy, mourning and praying,

I found myself.

Truth and love

will buy you the best gold mine known to mankind.

See, I have an innate tendency to deliver a unique experience

when cast into a scene of emotional, sexual correlation.

Should I say yes,

well to you sir

I then say,

God bless,

Because over here,

it will be one hell of a first.

"HOPE + STRIFE = POWERFUL"

MY LIGHT

I wish your sex would solve the mess I wrestle with in my head,

I'm a ghost in my body of late,

In what I'd call an emergency type of state,

And if you've ever wept for your lonely body and perpetuating

brokenness,

You can relate

To my upcoming recount of a night I light with words of lyrical

finesse,

Potent in sexual energy fit for a goddess

And peppered with intimate stress;

So, this is what happened

That trapped my insides in his mould:

I folded when he told my anatomy

To secrete emotional violations by historic lovers

And tear-jerking ecstatic emotions,

His fingers clutched my trembling situation,

Preventing any chance of convulsions,

I just had to remember to breathe,

Concentrated breathes as his mouth swallowed my pain and

delivered wet joys

I was a vision of overjoyed noise,

Far from poised

As I coiled into ecstasy,

This was beyond fantasy,

Fucking fanatically,

My lover was healing me like a provider,

Firing a bazooka inside my womb

I says I died yes,

Legs shook and he knew I was took,

So he took to deliver me to my creator,

Killed me.

My corpse was a limp picture of matter drenched in liquids,

Time, he offered my soul time in sublime,

Then resurrected me with a petal kiss on my lips,

I opened one eye,

Smiled

And decided he was my light.

For John

It's quiet,

The seas have calmed their nerves

and now you and I can walk on water,

No crashing of waves, high tides riding high overhead,

Stillness,

Things are different now,

Between you and I,

Not too many words fly between us,

They skip from mouth to ear and ear to mouth

In perfect amounts,

I still don't understand the sum of you

And which factor I am

Yet I am not worried anymore,

No anxiety about you leaving me untimely,

Just the peace of my peace of mind

I thought I had lost,

When you said that I was the cause,

I don't see you anymore

making me wonder about you all the more,

Is your head resting,

Is she keeping you happy,

And are the kids healthy,

But I carry on in distant caring

Careful not to disturb the settled storm,

And not to worry about how ugly

Things got so quickly

Because I did what I did

And you said what you said,

I still care;

So when The Roots sing their song

and it's your name I see on the screen,

My heart will smile,

Before my mouth says hello,

And we'll be on the phone,

Chatting all mellow,

Like friends who just saw each other

A whole minute ago

The People I Meet

And love,

They always leave you see,

Or they kill you.

> Must be damaged, confused or confusing,
>
> Please, no nice without an edge of fright,
>
> Lend me a dagger so I may joust with my lover,
>
> And pray no one kills the other,
>
> We're just playing sir,
>
> This is our game -
>
> Hostile, excited or exciting,
>
> Give me a sad comedian,
>
> I'll take a depressed dependent millionaire,
>
> Just keep the fool who has nothing to lose
>
> or knows not the feeling of losing everything;

Spit in my face first before you hand me

a man from some band, oh so grand,

Back off my land!

Your type is the worst,

I can't stand

At least I don't fade into a facade

Marching in a masquerade,

Launching grenades

At those with little aid

Attempting to hide my vulnerabilities as you exploit theirs,

Your kind, the worst.

yes,

Me, please give me,

Give me distorted, misunderstood;

Mind power elevating, we drink that ink that inebriates our
current state -

We always take the bait,

Laugh, cry, die and we rise,

Them and I,

at the end,

end up nude, raw and on the floor,

We all make for the door,

One by one, no whore stroll, no run,

although never fun,

We slowly leave

To be back and do it all again,

and it's never the same

Because every moment is a painful regression,

Always a different game.

These people, I have come to know

Love and they always leave you see

Or they just kill you.

"Still loving, feel myself getting better"

Remember Me.

Please, should the sun finally implode on itself

And the waters flush the land out,

And humans survive as animals in the veld,

Remember me

because I will be looking for you;

Should you find your love, marry, and live forever happy after,

Kids, cars and you give her the stars

because she is your world,

Remember me,

Because you are the world that I wish I could've had;

Should the lungs in your cavity steady and fail you,

And your vision blurs while your feet cannot carry you that

mile,

As your heart bleeds from open sores,

Remember me

Because I will be looking for you to carry you through;

Should friends wear thin, and materials end relationships,

While heads turn away from you

And everything dwindles to nothing,

Remember me

Because I will be your bread, butter and milk looking for you;

Should I find my prince, bear my kids, wearing a smile that

rivals moons,

And the life I dreamed, is no longer awake in my sleep

But the life I wake up to every day of my blessed life,

Remember me,

Because you are the love I never experienced

The love I fought for in my nightmares,

The love I wanted but never had,

The love that could've been the reality that I dreamed,

The one I wouldn't be writing to

Asking to be remembered,

Should the spin of the world remain as it is,

Remember me

Because I will never forget you.

I LOVE THIS MAN

There was never anything wrong with me

And in media-induced amnesia,

He is my reminder and my sense-provider,

That I,

Am doing just fine,

This man,

I love this man.

An Unexpected Impression

I was never impressed by the late nights

that dragged him in the bright hours of sunrise

as he carried the stench of stale shebeen air,

It never once impressed me,

And I let him know at the lateness of the afternoon

When he was the face of sobriety

And his eyes met mine without the glisten of Svedka;

It impressed me even less

when my voice of distaste for his late escapades

were met with a fury fist that colored my eye blue

and stained my blouse red;

You want to speak of impressed,

That man impressed me little,

In his temporary death,

Watching him so still, no snore, sweet sleep galore

He impressed me the most,

The man I married, under the impression

He would impress me infinitely, silly me;

I was never impressed by the waves of apologies

That drowned me after Sunday mass,

"Baby, I'ma change"

Never impressed,

"You are my queen"

Hardly impressed

And yet he pressed, on

Oh, how Sundays impressed me little,

Because come Monday,

Gone was God and on came Gin,

The mirror stood still and impressed me the least

Reflecting a painful truth,

Unimpressed,

why did I remain to live to never be impressed?

It's that reflection that shook the most

And impressed me the least,

Because it scold me,

That that man,

I could always leave.

I was never impressed

By the nights I had my bags packed,

keys in hand,

Only to sit and stay

With that man,

And the most,

I was never impressed

by me.

"Sex is not to be confused with love. Pain is not to be confused with love. Love is not to be confused with bad. Bad is not to be used as an excuse for sex and love."

Still!

The only problem is that I love him.

I left town,

Cancelled my connections,

loved other men,

I was happy alone,

Gave myself time,

I even forgot,

Until I saw him,

And I would have carried on

But you see mama,

He looked at me,

I saw him look at me

And he remembered me,

his hazel eyes had grown in intensity from the years past,

And I stirred in my core

wondering what that look meant,

My thoughts raced paralyzing me,

I couldn't tell you whether I smiled at him but I could not hold

my legs any longer,

Maybe I waved,

But I willed myself to move,

And before I could talk myself out of walking over

I was walking over to him

Past the pretty women and their pretty dresses,

Past the dashing men in their Bond suits,

Past the obstacles shoving champagne glasses in my face,

I was walking over to him as he to me,

In the center, I think it was there that we met

And he smiled

And his eyes poked me with their sparkle

And that thing somewhere deep in a dark place

That I swore I had buried,

Came alive,

like fireworks on July,

sparks started to fly.

I think he said hello or maybe it was hi

But in every bit of my biological make up,

It felt good to see him,

I wanted him to look at me like that for the rest of my forever,

I wanted to run away with him

And hide in secret kingdoms;

transform passion poetry to erotic motion reality

Until I was breathless and senseless

And he clothed me with his naked scent;

Even after those years,

The unnecessary pain emotions,

The boyfriends, lovers, wives, fiancés and kids,

I still!

Loved the man,

wanted to hold his hand in the morning sunshine

to the corner store

for a cup of one sugar, milk caffeine small coffee

and kiss our way back to the house

To begin the rest of our lives.

You Got Me

If I had to imagine,

if I had to secretly strip my inhibitions and bathe my body in oil

erotica,

what would become of me?

If Mother Mary from St. Mary's Catholic school went to bed

and Sister Jacobs' voice silenced itself in my head,

what animal would I be hiding?

I invite you tonight

to the happenings of last night,

and ask that you hold judgments steady

instead get ready

for the unraveling of my true identity

suppressed by Roman Catholics' indoctrination over years

past,

freed by the idea of liberty

and the sight of Timothy.

First, I begin with "shit!"

Apologies to Thy Father from up above,

But I simply need "shit" because you hid this surprise from my

eyes, mind and vagina.

Surprises never came in chiseled chests, tight vests with a

swagger

that pleases like some pleasure dagger.

I looked at the man trying not to drool,

His sweat seemed to drip in slow motion

and I began to imagine my body as his faithful devotion,

In my home space we were

And my head space had flown to some outer space

a space where clothes seem to relocate and things fascinate.

I summoned the six-foot Harlem king,

beckoned him with the look in my eyes

that spoke of sugar, spice and some nice surprise;

He looked like some delicious, decadent dish that had been

brewing in some pot

and now was ripe, ready and in my cot.

You put a piece of meat in front of me,

it's going into my mouth

that is the natural progression of such a situation;

And so it was,

my lips were his guide

into the sultry hollows of my mouth

where my tongue played with him in reverberating oscillations,

hence where he was dead before

he was now up and alive

and I knew he was feeling my vibe,

I could tell from the way his hands grabbed my waist

to the way he kissed my face,

I knew he wanted to do things to me,

things that I would like

things that I would love

things that would have me sitting in heaven up above.

Yet I craved him more,

wanted to give him more

have him sleeping in some sensual sexual situation galore,

We were lip-locked,

legs crossed

and I swear the room must have been shaking

from our insistent gyrating

as if there was an African Congo drum leading us on

to a silent fading.

I dripped all over him

and he splashed all over me

and I caught every single drop

but of course

he was the best lollipop,

we were slow in our lovemaking,

we fucked hard in our fucking

and we were that poetic justice in our soul connection.

Last night Timothy happened to my body

and I know I happened right back to his

and all I could say was,

'if you were worried about where...baby don't worry you know

that you got me"

He got me

and he got me good.

"If you have never swallowed your own bile in attempt to not regurgitate the pain from a broken heart, then you have not known that "in love" thing. Not to say that love hurts, it doesn't but to get to the right one, don't be alarmed by a little froggy discomfort. Get through that and you become the poetry."

You Want To

If I could fly,

I'd hide you in between wings

And hope angels don't ask about the devil peeking through my

feathers

Disrupting heaven's weather

Cause no matter

How bad and evil you act towards a sister,

Leaving you is to have never loved you

And that lie would cause my soul to die

And I'd rather die

At the hands of a lover I consider a soul provider,

Than suffer a moment without my butterfly creator type of

kisser;

I know it's been busy these past weeks between gigs,

dudes and chics lit over my poetry shit,

It seems like I'm getting ready to split

But pass the *spliff,*

Let's chill to the riff

And enjoy the gift hidden between slits

Made tight for your perfect fit.

I see that grin,

You too want to fly,

So fly with me.

Thieve

I've let you,

Unequivocally and completely allowed my bosom to console your

soul,

Rejuvenate you whole,

Rest your all in to my warm hole

Never to be forlorn,

By the time he was gone

And the sun caressed my eyelids to peep the morning screen,

I ceased to be the queen

I was called to be,

You see,

While you and I were asleep

You stole my oil to light your fire

And I let you,

I let that thing in me that ignites memories of a warm home with

mama's soft kisses

Escape my slip

And grip you gently into a needy little boy

That wanted more of No's core,

Leaving me dry,

I die,

I'm left alone;

In the fullness of your comfort

I'm famished,

Diminished

In a familiar ditch

Where a man has taken

More than to just explore,

And I let you,

Thieve my jewels:

I now see a boy who occupies a space

Where pain will make a man out of the fool you confuse as being one.

FOUND LOVE

Before I hit this mic,

Let me unwind what I have come to find

That there are some things a woman cannot say on a mic

But ask Mike what I can do when I do get on a mic.

I bet my womb will let you pick every stress, mess and pain

I ever knew

And you,

You beguiling, heavenly African god of my busty bosom blooming in

erectile excitement

Will invite gushes of streams

Resulting in screams

from my soul to pour from the corners of my dormant volcanoes that

only explode in spiritual revivals.

You,

Decadent devotee,

Are my revival,

Clothed in nude

I know you to be my truth,

So shhhh,

Let me take care of you,

You've known no woman 'till today

And I am all you will ever need to remember.

Phase 2:

I was made to bathe my babe in an amalgamation of sensual

sensations,

Cultivated by the ancestors that birthed Cleopatra herself,

The reach of my hips is no mistake

As we sway in rhythmic seduction,

Summoning the beast in you

To be tamed lame by the ferocity of my thighs,

The highs you and I would reach

Conquering mountain peaks

As we speak

In elevated bodily diction

Sketching eloquent fiction

- With our divine connection,

This section blesses erections

And it is only to be had if Spirituality sanctions;

And you, him,

He was all kinds of right

And there was never any inclination to put up a fight,

The chase was just to wet his appetite

And baste my insides

But I knew he would fit just right,

He was my light

That incinerated all the trash the years had left on my front yard

Staining my lawn like sores that stayed too long;

Spit shined this dime

And I claimed him as mine.

Phase 3

He saw, roared and came home.

And I caught every drop of this lion

And gave him time to acquaint his soul with the real deal.

It was quietly understood that he would be the one to carry me as I

carried the life that would one day carry us to our final resting days.

This was it,

This was Love.

Feminist

Before my last breath becomes the ledge with which heaven greets

my breast,

All I have to confess

I will express

And every man that ever made mess

All over my den

Leaving stains of stress on my dresses,

Pay attention please

For you never knew me;

I cook

clean,

fuck my dick

And let him call me a dirty little you know that nasty word

Word!

And still I am a feminist,

I'm just doing what's right;

Far from ashamed,

At loving the sight of my man's glock

I'd knock on any door

Shout from any rooftop

I love it!

James Wilson Jr.

I love your dick!

Yes,

Closed doors and four walls,

Neighbors don't know

how I turn tricks

Lick lips on fat sticks,

To then sit

And kill any spit that insists the nature of make up

Depletes my worth to sit at the table.

My Jamaican whine does not affect my ability to intellectually

grind

And fortify my place

In a world set against my sex and race,

I just know what a man needs;

I am a feminist,

though you should know

I come home before old folks' bones

Begin to ache,

To make sure your belly is fed by the hand that folds fists in the day

for rights,

And kneads bread for family by night;

You will always be alright

If you keep me at your right;

Carry my bags and I'll stroke yours,

Build me a house

And I'll make a home of it

That no whore would dare explore

For the us that you and I are

Is a sacred sanctitude that would discourage any indiscretion;

Man,

Strong, bold,

I understand you to the bone

Lay your head on my bosom

And let my soul Band-Aid your wounds

Let me stitch your cuts

From those junks

Who confused you with their bought goodies plastered on their bodies

With my real love,

And above all else

Let me rub your feet please

Because I need this

To please this

To appease this

This being,

Man that you are,

Let my insides explode in submission and explode all over your hard

parts;

Let this feminist do you right

All night

And let my bright light

Blind you to heaven

For even if they see a Badu-like concoction

There's no confusion

When it comes to you,

I see a king's reflection

And my daily affections

Are my sincerest of intentions

To simply love on you.

So, when this feminist

Snaps into a suit to fight continental wars

To dining with congressional folk behind fancy walls,

I never forget that

You

Are my king

And I am your queen.

Walk into the Light

I cannot say that I miss you,

That you violate my thoughts with the intrusion of your memory as

I'm making strides in my plight to forget you,

No.

I will not say that you camp out in black corners of my mental matter

scoffing at lovers who attempt the impossible

To love me like you did.

No sir.

I will not say your shit put others' shit to shame and used to maim

me to sleep in euphoric disbelief

That a body could experience such oscillating relief,

With you, no need for any s*pliff*

You were the peak to my riff.

No.

I will however

Write this piece as a ceremonial peace offering to the gods

To free the soul of my vagina

From mourning the loss of your rock,

How you rocked me steady initially to ultimately;

Knew my kinks and spread licks that locked me into a matrix so

complex

Sex meant your name,

Nothing was ever the same

And no man would ever eat from my plate.

Creature of God,

Delicious son of Universe,

I summon your bones to my present,

Now burn,

With this poem,

Let your ashes dissipate into air

Where even I can't try to find you

On days when your scent assaults my spirit into tears

Leaving me to rummage through texts, messages and papers for a

number to drag you back into my hole where you left me alone.

God I love you!

So please,

Power of words

With this I write and call to be

The end of this lover

Master of suckers

Free me as a prisoner.

As I deliver this literature,

I accept that I am your murderer.

Die baby.

God I love you!

A moment of silence for the ex-lover

Amen.

And as the end greets you

Rest easy

Knowing I'll be looking for you in year 2105

maybe then we can get it right

But for now,

walk into the light.

Exit

No matter what happens love never leaves…

I stood behind the bar at Starbucks in 2011 talking and laughing with one of my favorite regulars while making her soy latte just the way she liked it; Mary was in her early sixties at the time and she was giving me my weekly update about her beautifully active love life. At sixty something she had the glow of a sixteen-year-old as she spoke of her new love interest. As we joked, laughed and I listened intently, she said, "Let me tell you something, whether you are a teenager or you're my age, that feeling is still the same, you still get the butterflies and the giggles, it never changes." Boom! There it was, a powerful lesson of love from a veteran of its school. Time undoubtedly had thrown this woman against the wall back and forth, having her clasping her chest heaving and panting because of the ferocity with which pain can induce in one because of some relationship involving love, yet still she exuded an airy light of love and beauty.

To search for oneself in relationships failed or otherwise, is to embark on a journey that will ultimately deliver your best or worst version of yourself, which it is, is entirely up to you. We discover, love and live through the interactions we participate in.

To completely surrender yourself to the process of a relationship is to expose vulnerabilities that could asphyxiate you EXCEPT death always births something new. I still struggle with love after too much pain that has come from loves who swore they loved me. What I have come to find in thrusting and weaving myself like a child who has known no pain in these relationships is discovering better versions of myself.

I impart no specific advice to my audience, only that you look for yourself in every relationship that has failed you or otherwise because after all, when all is said and done, and you go to bed alone with just the air and your conscience, it's all about you. Whether there is a body next to yours or not, will you slip peacefully into sleep or will you standoff with insomnia wondering who in the world you are?

This book was never truly about sex, it was always about self-identity, the pleasures life has in store for you when you open yourself up to the notion of finding out, and then some. What you get is what you get. What I offer you is no more than love and soulful revelations in intimate situations as you live out the rest of your days.

FROM THE AUTHOR:

I would love to take this time to do my thank yous. Since you are reading this right now, it is only right I thank you first. So, thank you. I can only hope that you enjoyed reading this book more than I did writing it, not to imply that it wasn't a joy but it wasn't always roses and sunshine. I poured my heart and the rest of me into it and it may not be my best but it's everything I got.

Next, my lovers: THANK YOU. Yes, the use of capital letters was vital because I could've drawn inspiration from other women and men but understand this, that there is nothing more real and raw than sitting on the A train with the darkest shades you own hiding the bubbling tears as your hand delivers ink to the pad violently, passionately and sweetly because of the mess you got yourself into. To every man that I have wept for, loved, wasn't allowed to love, who never loved me back, woke up with hangovers for, lost my appetite for, was suicidal for, gave up on love because of them for, hated men because of them for, and was left almost completely empty because of them; It is these very men that have given me the brightest and darkest of experiences, I thank you.

My sister, *Thobeka: *uyityatyambo eyingavumi ukhufa, uthando lwakho liyandi vudumeza xandi godola, umama no tata sisi, wena, bayazi qenya ngawe.* You are what is left of the home that carries me through my endeavors and life, I do love you and I thank you for loving your way through people's blatant negativity, I get it.

My friends, family members, former classmates and strangers, thank you for encouraging me to live and share. And if you discouraged me, your role wasn't any less important, so I must thank you too. And my team, the team that help put this book together...there are no words truly

God, Thank You.

you are a flower that refuses to die, your love warms me when it's cold, mom and dad are proud of you

Nomxolisi Ndlangana, commonly known as Nono, is a native of South Africa; she moved to New York for education, its cultural variety and artistic inclination. She received her BA in Media Studies at Hunter College. Nono formally began her career as a performer in New York in 2011 as a spoken word artist hitting low key stages in Harlem to slamming at the internationally acclaimed Nuyorican Poets Cafe.

Nono has developed her artistry throughout the years, fusing her poetry with instrumentals and vocals, taking inspiration from blues, jazz and neo-soul which led to her first project, an EP titled Wet Paint. Her lyrics are simple projections of her social interests with a strong poetic tone. Soul Vagina is her debut poetry compilation. She still lives in New York, and splits her time between her book writing and performing.

Follow Nomxolisi "Nono" Ndlangana at:

NonoThePoet.com

Instagram.com/NonoThePoet

Facebook.com/NonoThePoet

Youtube.com/NonoThePoet

Twitter.com/NonoThePoet

www.ingramcontent.com/pod-product-compliance
Lightning Source LLC
Chambersburg PA
CBHW051845090426
42811CB00034B/2213/J